Travel Etiquette

Airports, Airplanes & About

Guidelines, Pandemic Travel Suggestions,
Checklist and Emergency First Aid

Michael Lynn
CEM, CME, CMM, CMP, CPC, CPEC

Dedication

To my wonderful and beautiful wife, Marcia. We have shared many trips together and she has endured my over fifty years of travel in the military and corporate world. This book would not have been possible without her drive and continuing inspiration in my life. She was my childhood sweetheart and still is. So, I take great pleasure in thanking and dedicating this book to Marcia.

Acknowledgements

Just the thought of writing a book makes my mind go into overdrive on how-to success in the process. Having a valuable group of individuals *(Super Friends)* can really help pull it all together. So, these are the ones that I would love to say were the driving force behind this book.

Carl Lester my flying buddy and friend for over 45 years. Most critical person you will find on anything. Will tell you straight up what he thinks and voiced several opinions *(attitudes)* about some of the subject matter and book design. We have traveled the world together in our Air Force and retirement days and value his opinion.

Colleen Rickenbacher who has been a key force in getting me to do this book and volunteering me for everything. She uses more red ink than my 11th grade English teacher. She has written several etiquette books including *"Be on your Best Business Behavior"* and is a professional speaker on all topics related to etiquette. Check out her books on Amazon and her website **www.crspeaks.com**.

Terry Sullivan *(The GURU of LinkedIn)* has been a motivator in how to move forward with the book and using social media to publicize. He is a great Speaker / Trainer and check him out at. **www.buzzpro.com**

Linda Swindling with her *"Passport to Success"* books that were a hit, provided me the thought that maybe I could write something similar for Protocol and Etiquette. Since then, she has written several great books such as *"Ask Outrageously."* Check her out on Amazon or here website: **www.lindaswindling.com** and **www.lindaswindling.com/Bookstore/**

Patricia Sanders a friend that is the leading professional in marketing and communications. She is an expert in how to make the material standout and best words to use. I value her ongoing support to always help me improve.

Edward Scannell *(The Professional Voice)* has been a motivator in just get out there and do it. Every time we talked, he was always motivating me to become a speaker and writer. He has authored numerous books and check him out on Amazon

Terry Matthews-Lombardo is what I call my guru in punctuation. Gave me tips in how to remember what to use where and why. She has a great travel blog **What Travel Was and Will Be – Terry's World Travels (terrysworldtravels.com)** and her new book *"Meetings Mayhem"* on Amazon is a must read.

Cynthia McDowell who I met through Protocol Diplomacy International – Protocol Officers Association (PDI-POA). She has given input and asked questions on numerous areas and her inputs have been valuable. To get her point across she uses little P.s that usually start with *under no circumstance should you …* that would be horrible.

Certifications

The Initials behind Michael's name represent the following industry certifications

CEM - Certified Exhibition Manager

CME - Certified Manager of Exhibitions

CMM - Certified Meeting Manager

CMP - Certified Meeting Planner

CPC - Certified Protocol Consultant

CPECP - Certified Protocol, Etiquette, Civility, Professional

Awards

"Top 40 over 40" Event Professional - SPIN,

"Protocol Professional of the Year" - PDI-POA,

"Exhibit Marketer/Manager Year"

> *EXPO Group and E2MA,*

"Top 5 Exhibit & Event Managers Worldwide"

> *Exhibitor Magazine,*

"Red Carpet Award for Exceptional VIP Service"

> *U.S.A.F.*

Contents

Chapter 1: Introduction

Airports, Airplanes & About Etiquette

Airport, Airplane *(travel)* Etiquette has gone out the window. People have lost their humanity, civility, good manners, common sense, when traveling. Have you noticed the line breakers / inhibitors, drag the refrigerator down the aisle, smelly / grease foodie connoisseur, grizzly bear snorer, arm rest hog, laptop / food tray crusher, there are several at every airport and on every flight?

In 2021, there has been over **5000** acts of violence, aggression, fighting, hostility, brutality, cruelty, incivility, rudeness, impoliteness, discourtesy on aircraft.

You can help by being nice, courteous, helpful, and maybe incorporating some of the following.

Let's start with some simple items on Airport, Airplane Etiquette and hopefully make the experience pleasant and enjoyable for all.

Your best chance of experiencing a flawless, less stressful travel experience comes with careful preparation.

The travel items I reference for use are to make your travel experience hopefully more pleasant and will all be listed at the end of the book. *(Items to Purchase for Your Travel.)* I want to stress I receive no compensation for anything I recommend in the book. These are items I have used and seen that work.

FIRST, be polite when communicating with travel personnel (*airlines, trains, cruise ships, buses*), crew members, and yes attendants are qualified crew members and there for your safety, not to cater to your whims, and please avoid taking up too much of their time. Do not forget the **"Please,"** **"Excuse Me,"** and **"Thank You"**.

NOT obeying an order from an airline crew member is a federal offense as noted:

Title 49 U.S.C.§46504. Interference with flight
crew members and attendants

An individual on an aircraft in the special aircraft jurisdiction of the United States who, by assaulting or intimidating a flight crew member or flight attendant of the aircraft, interferes with the performance of the duties of the member or attendant or lessens the ability of the member or attendant to perform those duties, or attempts or conspires to do such an act, shall be fined under title 18, imprisoned for not more than 20 years, or both. However, if a dangerous weapon is used in assaulting or intimidating the member or attendant, the individual shall be imprisoned for any term of years or for life.

Almost any offensive or disruptive **behavior that distracts the crew** *can be considered interference, such as*

- *disobeying repeated requests to sit down, return to your seat, or turn off an electronic device.*
- *To avoid trouble or possible arrest:*
- *Please do as you are asked.*
- *Be respectful and please do not raise your voice or make threats.*
- *If there is a problem ask to speak with the Senior Flight Attendant, ask for Airline officials, security, local law enforcement to meet aircraft.*
- *Never, ever touch a crewmember or any person, that can be considered assault.*

*As a warning you may be handed a **"Passenger Disturbance Notice"**, that explains the law.*

Note: *You should never feel you were inconvenienced or had to stop eating something you loved. However, when using public transport of any kind, you should be mindful of how your actions might affect others*

CASE IN POINT *--- **ALLERGIES** --- are real and different things affect individuals in different ways. Some people can react violently **(even die)** from the mere existence of something in the air (e.g., peanuts), others it can be a strong perfume / cologne smell that may cause respiratory problems. Just be mindful.*

If you see a service person (*military, fireman, police, first responders*), buy them a meal, give them a better seat, gift card to a food / coffee facility at the airport, say **"Thank You."** (*I buy a few gift cards when I arrive and pass out as needed. There are many of the same chain restaurants at all major airports.*)

"Remember
There's no such thing
As a small act of **KINDNESS***.*
Every **ACT** *creates a ripple*
With no logical end."
~ Scott Adams

Chapter 2: Travel During A Pandemic / Disaster

(Epidemic, Plaque, Virus, COVID, National /Worldwide Disaster, Flu Season)

If you must travel during any worldwide situation the key is to be **INFORMED** and **PREPARED**. Your responsibility during any situation is to follow and comply with government restrictions, especially when related to travel.

1. The CDC has recommended travellers to **AVOID ALL NONESSENTIAL TRAVEL** during any outbreak. Be advised that in other countries you may have limited access to adequate medical care.

2. Numerous countries with little advanced notice **may implement travel restrictions, mandatory quarantines, border closing, and not allowing non-citizens entry.**

3. Airlines worldwide **may change flights daily** and this can make travel unpredictable. **Be aware** that your travel plans can be disrupted and your entry into the United States or any other country could be delayed indefinitely.

There are **numerous websites** to check for information, prior to your travel, regarding the **COVID-19, Immunization Requirements, Country Advisories / Restrictions**.

Stay **UP-TO-DATE** and **INFORMED.**

The CDC *(center for disease control)* **website provides info on the following areas related to the current COVID – 19 outbreaks.**

https://www.cdc.gov/coronavirus/2019-ncov/ travelers/index.html

1. Coronavirus and Travel in the United States.

2. Returning from International Travel.

3. Travelers Prohibited from Entry to the United States.

4. Travelers Returning from Cruise Ship and River Cruise Voyages.

5. COVID-19 Travel Recommendations by Country.

6. Travel: Frequently Asked Questions and Answers.

U.S. State Dept
https://travel.state.gov/content/travel/en/
traveladvisories/traveladvisories.html

D.H.S. *(dept homeland security)*
https://www.dhs.gov/

W.H.O. *(world health organization)*
https://www.who.int/

T.S.A *(transportation security administration)*

Always check before you go on what is allowed in 3-1-1-quart plastic bag.

- 3.4 ounces (100.55ml) or less per container

- 1 quart size, clear, plastic, zip top bag (all liquids must fit in bag)

- 1 bag per passenger

TSA is allowing one liquid hand sanitizer container up to 12 ounces (354ml) per passenger in carry-on bags **<u>until further notice</u>**. Passengers can expect that these containers larger than the standard allowance of 3.4 ounces (100.55ml) of liquids permitted through a checkpoint **<u>will need to be screened separately (in a Ziplock bag)</u>**, which will add some time to their checkpoint screening experience.

Please keep in mind that all other liquids, gels and aerosols brought to a checkpoint continue to be allowed at the limit of 3.4 ounces (100.55ml) carried in a one quart-size bag.

https://www.tsa.gov/travel/security-screening/
whatcanibring/items/hand-sanitizers

Check with your Airport and see if they have a COVID-19, Pandemic, or Disaster Website.

Check with your Airline

    a. Flights

    b. Terminals open

    c. Clubs open

    d. Airplane procedures

    e. Can you bring food and beverage, *(must still meet TSA guidelines).*

    f. MASK requirements

Traveling Method / Means / Mode…

(Airline, cruise ship, train, bus).

At present Air Travel is taking a major hit on mode of travel due to the COVID-19 virus and will for a period of time.

There may even be new permanent travel guidelines for the future.

So always check with your mode of travel company and departure location on current guidelines / procedures.

Over the past several decades viruses *(flu, H1NI, Ebola)*, can and do spread faster due to global air travel.

Airplanes / Airports Cleanliness and Air Quality

At present, Airports and Airlines are doing extensive cleaning of their facilities and aircraft daily.

I suggest antibacterial wipes to clean everything around you, *(seat, tray table, armrest, air vent, entertainment touch screen, window, window shade, panel next to window, lavatory).*

Remember other items when traveling that you may need to clean *(baggage bin at TSA, handrails or doors on shuttles, elevator buttons, hotel room; remote's – phone – hair dryer – safe – clothes hangers – thermostat, etc.).*

Several individuals have contacted me regarding the quality of air on aircraft. *(Guess since I spent 20 years as a flight crew member, I might know a few things about aircraft.)*

There's a common misconception that "**recirculated air**" in **airplanes** makes people more likely to get sick. In modern **planes**, that simply isn't true. Nowadays, **airplanes** have hospital-grade HEPA (high efficiency particle arresters, 99%), filtering systems that entirely recirculate the air in the cabin entirely every three to four minutes. You can check with your mode of transportation on their systems.

Focusing on air travel however, as with any flu season, there are precautions you can take to minimize your risk of becoming unwell.

Sick Or Have a Temperature

Protect yourself and others by not traveling when you are sick or have a temperature. Numerous airports worldwide are conducting health screening checks on arriving, transiting, and departure passengers.

Be prepared that you could be denied boarding for just having a fever.

Vaccinations / Shot Record

While in the military I had to carry a Shot Record with all vaccinations I currently had received.

Best advice is to <u>check with your medical doctor on required immunizations for your travels especially international</u> <u>and you might ask about having some form of a shot record.</u>

Keeping vaccinations up-to-date can help you stay healthy and prevent your immune system from compromise. It is also recommended that you get an annual **Flu Shot** but always check with your medical doctor.

Website for visiting country of travel for additional information.
https://wwwnc.cdc.gov/travel/page/travel-vaccines

Vaccination chart for adults 19 years of age or older.
https://wwwnc.cdc.gov/travel/

Vaccination chart for Birth to 18 Years of age.
https://www.cdc.gov/vaccines/schedules/hcp/imz/adult.html

Good Hygiene

Be mindful of Good Hygiene. Take a shower / bath before any trip and be mindful of using heavy deodorants / perfume / cologne due to people's sensitivities and allergies.

Eat a good meal before you travel *(at the airport)*. Suggestion: buy a gift card for a service member, first responder, and say ***"THANK YOU"***.

Before you board the mode of transportation **"GO TO THE RESTROOM AND TAKE YOUR CHILDREN"** *(help eliminate some of the exposure during the travel)*.

Hands

Perform hand hygiene frequently, particularly after contact with respiratory secretions *(nose, mouth especially, but be mindful of eyes)*.

Hand hygiene includes either cleaning hands with soap and hot water *(20 seconds)* or with an alcohol-based hand rub or wipe. Alcohol-based hand rubs are preferred if hands are not visibly soiled.

Especially clean your hands after TSA Check point, everyone is touching those bins.

Touching Face

Avoid touching your mask, mouth, nose, eyes with unwashed hands, as viruses most frequently enter the body through these routes.

Mask

Most airlines and numerous facilities, business, cities, are requiring the use of a face mask. Know before you **GO**.

Masks are effective in blocking, or at least limiting, your exposure to contagious viral droplets and aerosol particles *(most common usually from coughing or sneezing)*.

Because we do not always know who is infected *(many coronavirus cases are asymptomatic; presenting no symptoms of disease)*, you should also wear a mask to protect others.

The N95 mask with an external valve is made to allow breathing easier. However, these type N95 masks maybe an issue. San Francisco Department of Health has stated that if an N95 mask has an external valve, it does not do an adequate job of protecting others who come near the wearer. If that person should cough or sneeze through the valve, unfiltered droplets could travel through the opening and potentially contact anyone in range. These masks are not allowed under the city's directive.

So, simply put a surgical or cloth mask over the N95 mask with an external valve and it can be salvaged for pandemic use.

There are numerous brands of N95 respirators mask on the market, be careful when purchasing making sure they are certified by **NIOSH** (national institute for occupational safety and health), so that you filter at least

95% of airborne particles. *(Two of the best companies for mask are 3M and Honeywell, but do your research.)*

Follow best practices on how to wear, remove, dispose of mask *(rubber gloves),* and on hand hygiene after removal.

Eye Glasses

Everyone is looking at covering the mouth and nose, but what about the eyes. If you don't want to wear a face shield or googles here are a few suggestions.

1. Wear your eye or sun glasses. *(Keep old prescription glasses as spares in your travel case.)*

2. Even if you don't wear glasses you can get a pair of the cheap reading glasses with no magnification.

3. You can also go to amazon.com or any home improvement store and purchase safety glasses and they have some very stylish clear and sun glasses that have added feature of wrapping around the eyes.

Hand Sanitizer / Wipes

Get in the habit of having both of these items with you at all times, in your bag, vehicles, office, home.

Brushing Teeth / Mouthwash

Not saying that this helps but it can't hurt to brush your teeth and use mouthwash often. Dentist are now having you gargle when you sit in the chair as a precaution.

Upgrade Your Seat / Select Window Seat

Upgrading your seat to business or first class on any of the modes of transportation, will allow a little extra personal space and less contact with other passengers. The same is true for a window seat that keeps you away from foot traffic and contact with other passengers.

Food And Drink

Check with your mode of transportation on what is allowed in the way of food and drink while traveling and if they will be offering anything. Will you be allowed to remove your mask during the trip? As for any travel, travellers are also advised to follow proper food hygiene practices.

Drink Bottle with extended drinking straw: https://m.media-amazon.com/images/I/61Ur7lht2YL._AC_UL480_FMwebp_QL65_.jpg

This may allow drinking without removing masks. Be mindful that drinking while traveling may require more lavatory / restroom trips.

Travel Insurance

Insurance companies' policies vary greatly. Most exclude coverage for pandemics and epidemics and other items, so please read the entire policy including fine print carefully and if any questions check with the issuing company.

I still recommend travel insurance for medical, trip interruptions, cruises, emergency medical flights, etc. and insurance that covers my luggage. *(Check with your mode of transportation of what they cover and limits.)*

Many sacrifices already have been made to control the epidemic.

LET'S MAKE SMART CHOICES NOW!

Chapter 3: Before You Go

1. Check that you have an approved ID *(identification)*

    Real ID-Compliant U.S. Driver's License – starting October 1, 2020 every air traveler 18 years of and older will need a state-issued enhanced driver's license or an approved / acceptable form of ID *(passport, etc.)* to fly within the United States.

    Check with your state on what their STAR looks like on the Driver's License

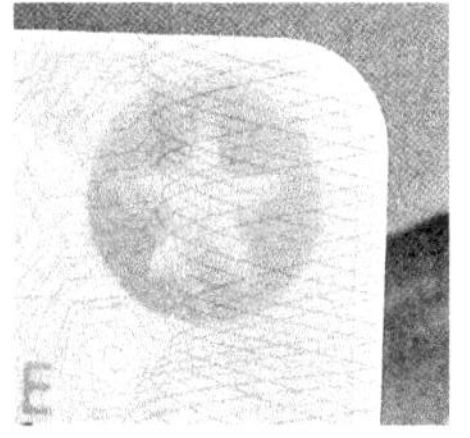

    (**Suggestion**, *when renewing driver's license ask that your state require a U.S. Birth Certificate, proof of U.S. Citizenship to obtain a U.S. Driver's License. Write to your congressman requesting this be the law.*)

2. Check with TSA for Items you can bring. https://www.tsa.gov/travel/security-screening/ whatcanibring/al-l

3. Purchase TSA approved locks. *(See items at end of book.)*

4. Register for Trusted Traveler TSA Pre✓® Program *(cost $85 U.S. for 5 years)*. **https://www.tsa.gov/ precheck**

    Frequently Asked Questions *(FAQ) TSA* **https:// www.tsa.gov/precheck/faq**

5. Register for **Global Entry**, is best to have, and also includes TSA Pre✓® Program above *(cost $100 U.S.)*. **https://www.cbp.gov/travel/trusted- traveler-programs/global-entry/how-apply**

6. Get Apps for flight tracking *(but always check the airport monitors – Most-Up-To-date before you get on the tram to the wrong gate)*, weather, your airline, hotel, rental car.

7. Setup up your phone with tracking so family knows where you are at.

8. Register for the Airline, Hotel, Vehicle Parking, Rental Car companies' loyalty programs that you will be utilizing the most. Building loyalty and status provides you with additional benefits *(upgrades, perks, change options, early / late check-out, etc.)*. Priority to selected seats on aircraft for Priority Status club members.

9. When booking your flight look at the type of aircraft you are flying on and check **www.SeatGuru.com** to pick the best seat on the plane.

10. Decide the best time of day to travel *(later in day*

offers less options for any flight cancellations or delays).

11. If you are looking for a cheaper flight, but has a layover *(how long is layover, are there additional flights if disruptions occur, most times direct flight is better).*

12. Tip / Gratuity Funds – Please tip service personnel, shuttle drivers, porters, etc. *(When traveling international I suggest getting some local currency at your departure airport so you are not caught short on arrival if no exchange facility available.)*

13. Credit Cards – your choice but get ones that work at most locations worldwide and notify them when you are traveling, especially international travel. *(I suggest two cards, one on you, and one in special carry-on location.)*

14. Computer Virus protection systems and good firewall. *(I like **www.stopzilla.com** and **https:// www.malwarebytes.com**/, I actually have both on my system. Have a strong firewall and passwords. I recommend Upper / lowercase letters, numbers, special characters and a minimum 10 digits.)*

15. I recommend small gifts for staff you will be interfacing with. *(I carry some small boxes of Godiva, writing pen that lights up at night—order some that say "Thank You" on them and not your company logo, etc.)*

16. Phone, invest in a good protected case, impact and water resistance.

17. Charge **ALL** your electronics. Remember the **A-B-C** of electronics, Always **Be** Charging.

18. Pictures. Make a picture of everything; luggage, parking spot with your vehicle, parking stub, valet stub, checked luggage stubs, taxi or car service you get in.

19. Three thing you never pass-up. **Water – Food – Bathroom.**

*"Your **Smile** is your **Logo**,*

*Your **Personality** is your **Business Card**,*

*how **you leave others feeling** after an experience with you becomes your **Trademark.**"*

~ Sam Glenn

Chapter 4: Pack Appropriate

First, pack appropriately for luggage that will go with you on the plane. Don't overpack, **PACK WHAT YOU NEED AND WILL USE.**

If you would like to skip having to take your carry-on, checked baggage, and sporting equipment you can send any ahead of time with **Shipgo**, and have it available at your destination. Check them out at.

https://www.shipgo.com/

1. Buy appropriate good quality luggage *(check reviews on best for checked and carry-on; TravelPro Crew, Delsey, are good, I also like a 4-wheel bag to eliminate stress on my arms by pulling)*, that meets requirements for overhead storage. Not all bags that are labeled for airline use fit in the overhead compartment *(get a lockable type just to be safe if it has to be checked)*. Domestic Standard size is 22" tall, x 14" wide, x 9" thick *(55.88cm, 35.56cm, 22.86cm)* including handle and wheels.

   a. Check your airline's websites on their size and weight limits.

> b. International travel has different rules, so again check with airline on size and weight. *(Airlines, like Qantas, Singapore, have a carryon weight of 15lbs / 7Kgs and they weigh them. The combined weight of your bag and laptop may put you over the limit and have to be checked.)*

2. Shuttle Flights *(small regional aircraft)*, be prepared that your carryon luggage will be checked at the gate.

3. One bag, with change of clothes *(pack light)*, and your 3-1-1 bag, and items you need.

   a. The **3-1-1 Rule** refers to three core components that govern how many liquids you can bring in your carry-on bags: Each liquid must be in a 3.4-ounce (100.55ml) or less container (3), all containers must be placed inside one (1) clear **quart-sized** plastic bag, and each passenger is only allowed one (1) plastic bag.

   b. Carry **ONLY** what **YOU** are allowed, 3-1-1, and check with airlines on other items. **https://www.tsa.gov/**

4. One bag *(briefcase, small backpack)* for your travel documents, computer, headset, book, etc., this is the one that goes under the seat in-front of your seat. Yes, ladies a purse counts as one of the two items.

Ladies you may want to look into a bag that works as purse and for electronic items *(laptop, headphones; check reviews on best for carry-on, TravelPro, Delsey).*

5. Identification on bag and inside. *(Don't use full name, company name or phone number.)*

    a. Securing your luggage, use a lock that secures the zippers to the handle. *(Most zippered luggage can be opened when locked.)*

    b. Order a lockable luggage strap with your **Initials Only** or a nickname.

    c. Use a Luggage Tag that **secures your name inside** the tag so it can't be read without taking it off. *(Don't use a business card with a company name or logo.)*

    d. For identification inside checked luggage. I suggest a card *(laminated)* with Name *(initials and last name only)*, Phone number (#) of family member.

6. Identification on Electronic Items. I suggest a card *(laminated on item)* with Name *(initials and last name only)*, Phone number (#) of family member.

7. Some more experienced travelers have the rule "Never Check Your Bag," this takes practice and discipline to actually work.

Note, good to have a few items that you might pass out to children that need something during flight *(coloring book*

/ crayons, book, small game, deck of cards. Dollar stores can make you a life saver and hero to everyone).

Note, for parents with small children make a goodie bag for passengers near you *(ear plugs, some candy / gum / mints, snack bar --* **no peanuts** *-- along with a note card with child's name saying something cute, "I'm _____ this is my first flight, and I may not be well mannered all the time. Please excuse me for any inconvenience, but trying to start early on getting frequent flyer miles").*

Special Note: Be Prepared for LOST Luggage

Make a picture of **ALL** your luggage and use your computer to add dimensions, type, cost, etc. and have it with you. It is valuable to incorporate with you lost luggage claim paperwork. *(Retaining the actual receipt for the purchased luggage will help in filing a claim, carry picture on your phone.)*

"We are all born rude. No infant has ever appeared yet with the grace to understand how inconsiderate it is to disturb others in the middle of the night.

~ **Judith Martin (aka Miss Manners)**

"Children are natural mimics
who act like their parent's
despite every effort to teach them good manners."

~ **Mark Twain**

Chapter 5: Need Wheelchair / Special Assistance

1. If you need assistance at airport *(wheelchair, etc.)* contact the airlines before you travel *(at least 48 hours, earlier even better).*

2. If person taking you to / from airport needs to assist you they can request an **escort pass.** *(Contact your airlines 48 hours prior for this service. Not all airlines provide escort passes at all airports.)* **ALWAYS** Plan on **NOT** receiving Escort Pass.

3. Passengers with disability or medical condition call ahead to TSA (855) 787-2227.

4. Plan additional time *(arrive very early, you may have to wait for wheelchair attendant).*

5. Inform your attendant of what you can and cannot do before arriving at security.

6. Check-in and go through security *(do not plan that you will get head of line privileges).*

7. Have plenty of **TIP / GRATUITY** funds. *(Suggestion is $10 U.S. dollars per 15 minutes of time, if they do extra then tip extra.)*

8. Choose larger aircraft for travel *(more reserved seating and restroom options, airlines may have restrictions on number of special assistance passengers per plane, so plan early)*. As a precaution I suggest wearing items if restroom is not available in time *(wearing Depends, Always, etc.)*. **"GO TO THE RESTROOM PRIOR TO BOARDING".**

9. Plan your meals *(wheelchair attendants are **NOT** required to take you to a restaurant or fast food, but required to take you to restroom)*.

10. If you need a wheelchair to board, you will probably board first but in an airplane approved wheelchair. Expect to check your personal wheelchair.

11. If you are checking your wheelchair, make sure to have instructions on how to disassemble if needed. *(Plan that it will always be checked.)*

12. Request a wheelchair on arrival when you make your initial reservation.

13. Plan ahead and have someone meet you at baggage claim.

14. You will not deplane until other passengers are off the aircraft.

15. If you have any problems, ask to speak to airlines Complaints Resolution Official (CRO).

"Life be not so short but that there is always time for courtesy."

~ Ralph Waldo Emerson

Chapter 6: Check-In

1. Check-in online and print your boarding pass before you go *(have your reservation booking number)*.

    If you are **TSA Approved** make sure it **prints** on your ticket.

2. Arrive two (2) hours before departure for domestic flights, and three (3) hours for international flights. Due to the COVID situation, it is advisable to check-in three (3) hours or more before all flights.

3. Know your terminal check-in before arrival.

4. If you check luggage curbside there usually is an additional per bag fee by the airlines. *(Tip your porter additional $1 to $2 per bag, especially if heavy.)*

5. Know the weight limits *(usually 50lbs, 22.6kg)*.

6. Secure your luggage *(do you know a locked zipper bag can be opened and resealed without you knowing it)*.

7. Identification on **OUTSIDE** of your bag.   Use

secure luggage tags. Use Initials and last name, phone number (#) only.

8. Identification for INSIDE your bag and laminated: Name, different address *(family member, office, etc.)*, phone number (#).

"Three things in human life are important

The First is to **BE KIND**

The Second is to **BE KIND**

And the Third is to **BE KIND."**

~ Henry James

Chapter 7: TSA / Security

1. Register for Global Entry and get on approved TSA Pre✓® system for expedited screening *(only at participating airports)*. When you print or receive your ticket *(check **TSA** appears on ticket)*.

2. Passengers with disability or medical condition always call ahead to TSA (855) 787-2227.

3. Try and fly at less popular times *(lines shorter)*.

4. Be **polite** and **cooperative.**

5. Listen and follow directions of TSA Officials.

6. Have the appropriate ID – if you are using a U.S. Driver's License states are changing Driver Licenses and you may need a new one. *(See **Real ID** under Before You Go.)*

7. Get a Passport *(you never know when you will need one)*.

8. Wear items that make the Security process easier.

    a. Shoes that come on / off easy, with socks – no bare feet *(No Flipflops)*. If you have to use the emergency slide your need your feet protected.

b. Clothing without metal in it. Less jewelry is better.

9. Be ready

a. Have ID, ticket / boarding pass available before you enter the TSA Line (*in a zippered or carry-on pocket*).

b. **Before** you enter the **Security Line**. Stop and remove loose items that will have to be taken off and put in a plastic gallon zip lock bag in your carry-on (*reduces the chance you will leave something in security bin*).

    i. Watch
    ii. Phone (*unless using for ticket, but always have a paper copy*)
    iii. Belt
    iv. Keys
    v. Loose change
    vi. Jewelry (*please do not wear expensive jewelry on a trip - Security*)

c. Have your phone, laptop, iPad, e-reader, CPAP machine, camera, any electronic items and 3-1-1 bag in outside pocket of carry-on for easy access.

Note: Electronic items need to be in screening

bin with nothing under or on top of item *(usually one per bin)*.

Note: Mark all your electronic items *(suggest not using your full name, but phone number (#), ok)*.

10. As you approach the screening checkpoint, remove outer garments *(jackets, sweaters, scarfs, shoes with buckles, belts, etc., and be ready to place in bin)*.

    If you know something is going to set off the detectors then take it off.

11. Remember to get all your items *(good reason to have items in gallon plastic bag)*.

**"Good manners sometimes means
simply putting up with other people's bad manners."**

~ H. Jackson Brown, Jr.

Chapter 8: Waiting Area

1. Avoid dependency on public **Wi-Fi** *(not secure and uses a lot of your data plan, download before you go)*.

2. Handicap seats are just for that.

3. General seating is for everyone, you use one seat and carry-on items go on the floor in-front of you.

4. Pickup and dispose of trash *(cleanup after yourself - everywhere)*.

5. Be mindful of what is going on around you. Remember the 3"S" system *(Security, Scams, Safety)*.

6. Have a small power cord that allows several items to be charged at once *(helps everyone)*.

7. **A-B-C** of Charging electronics. **A**lways **B**e Charging.

8. **GO TO THE RESTROOM AND TAKE YOUR CHILDREN *(BEFORE BOARDING).***

"Rudeness is the weak man's imitation of strength."

~ Eric Hoffer

Chapter 9: Airline Clubs

If you only travel a couple of times a year then airline clubs maybe an expensive perk for your travels *(daily pass maybe better use of funds)*. A few options that can help in your decision process.

1. Clubs provide an extra level of security.

2. Check on the locations you will be using most frequently with the airline and see if they are available.

3. Most airlines when flying First or Business Class for **International** Flights allow free access. However, flying First or Business Class inside U.S. usually requires club membership. Some airlines have separate lounges for each class of service *(they also may have lounge access with their partners, but check)*.

4. Peace and Quiet *(will allow you to relax, stretch, comfortable seating, and even work)*.

5. Great work environment *(desk, power outlets, printers)*.

6.   Access to Airline Staff *(help with anything, and readily available)*.

7.   Snacks and Drinks *(at some locations you may receive free drink coupons, please don't over indulge and remember to **TIP**)*.

8.   Check out Priority Pass for their cost *(over 1300 lounges)*. Check your airport and travel location.

9.   Day Pass – good if delayed for extended period *(but check with your airline and airport)*. **Note:** *During unforeseen major airport delays, airlines may not allow day pass option.*

10. Check with your airline for a credit card that allows club access, while also accumulating those frequent flier miles and other benefits. *(Look at American Express Platinum – gives you access to several different airline lounges.)*

11. Club Members Guide.

   a. Be polite.

   b. Watch where you store luggage *(security)*, and place in club area.

   c. Be mindful of seating *(luggage stays on the floor not in a seat)*.

   d. Charge your electronics. Remember the **A-B-C** of electronics, **A**lways **B**e **C**harging.

   e. Be conscious of <u>voice / sound levels</u> on ringtones *(silent mode, with vibrate is best)*, and when talking on any phone. *(NEVER discuss classified, sensitive, private, company, personal info on any phone call.)*

f. Clean up after yourself.

g. Tip staff.

h. **GO TO THE RESTROOM BEFORE YOU LEAVE.**

"Good manners will open doors that the best education cannot."

~ Clarence Thomas

Chapter 10: Wear Appropriate Clothing

1. Wear appropriate clothing, comfortable and loose fitting works best. *(Helpful during an emergency or sitting on the plane for long periods. Forget the flip-flops, high heels, halter tops, tank tops, bathing suits, short pants / skirts. If you have to evacuate the plane you will want the shoes, and unprotected skin is going to get slide burns, and outside the plane could be cold, wet weather or hot surfaces.)*

2. I am not saying you have to wear a suit and tie for men or a long stylish dress for ladies, but think versatility. Color coordinate *(one color palate)* and multipurpose items that can be dressed up or down. This will also help eliminate the need for additional pairs of shoes.

   Note: I like to wear a nice pair of jeans *(usually dark, with no holes or worn spots)* with a dark black / blue jacket. The jacket I have coordinated to go with my suit pants, gray / khaki slacks, jeans and shoes. Basically, can dress for any occasion.

3. If airlines are looking to upgrade passengers, the nicer dressed may have a slight advantage. *(Do not dress like you are going to the beach, gym, jogging.)*

"Good manners are just a way of showing other people that we have respect for them."

~ Bill Kelly

Chapter 11: Personal Hygiene & Other Considerations

1. Take a bath / shower and use appropriate deodorant *(not heavy on anything smelly – people have allergies / sensitivities).*

2. Don't do personal hygiene on the plane *(this is not the place to trim / polish your nails, apply makeup, perfume / cologne, or hairspray).*

3. **NO PDA** *(personal display of affection).* It is unbelievable what I have seen on planes *(get a room).* The restroom / lavatory is cramped and unlikely to be very clean, so it is inappropriate to join the Mile-High Club *(who came up with that name)* and expose yourself to germs.

4. If you are a large person, then consider purchasing two seats *(required on some airlines now, do not wait and be embarrassed on the aircraft, especially if the armrest is in the fixed position).* I would like to use all of my seat and the armrest, not share it with you.

*"Do the right thing.
Even when no one is looking
It is called INTEGRITY."*

~ C.S. Lewis

Chapter 12: Items to Carry with You

(See Suggestion List at end.)

1. Pillow / blanket. I suggest a neck support item for short flights and the pillow *(MyPillow* **https://www.mypillow.com/** *has a new travel pillow that rolls up)* for long flights. *(Jacket can replace a blanket.)*

2. Beach ball. *(I know your laughing, but this works. Inflate the ball to a comfortable size, lay a blanket / jacket over it and you can lay your head into it to sleep and relieves the stress on your back, or put up next to the window. Grab some at Dollar Store when picking up a few items to pass out to children.)*

3. Eye sleep mask.

4. Ear plugs or noise cancelling headset, also, headphones for any electronics including phone. *(No Wireless or Bluetooth types, all should plug into the device you are using.)*

5. Food / drink *(not smelly, messy).*

6. Chewing gum (*good to relieve pressure in the ears*). breath mints (*refresh from that scrumptious post-airplane-meal breath*).

7. Charger (*do not forget cables and appropriate international plug, check with airline on what is available at your seat, flight attendants don't provide*). **A-B-C** of electronics, **A**lways **B**e **C**harging.

8. Portable power bank (*solar power/chargeable is good*).

9. Power cord (*great so you can plug all items into one*).

10. Smoke mask. (*The oxygen mask on the plane provides life sustaining oxygen, but* **DOES NOT** *filter out smoke. So, if oxygen is used just put the mask on over your oxygen mask, also good to have for hotel fire.*)

11. Sanitized wipes / gel (*remember 3-1-1 rules on liquids*)

12. Lotion not scented (*skin dries out at altitude, 3-1-1 rule*).

13. Sunblock not scented (*use it, you are getting more than you think at altitude, 3-1-1 rule*).

14. Rain poncho (*small clear plastic – no logos*).

15. Roll compressed toilet paper (*laugh again until you need it, especially on arrival in other countries*). Check Amazon.

16. Sleep aids – Over the counter or doctor prescribed.

17. Glasses, eye / sun *(keep those old prescription glasses as a backup in your bag).*

18. Eye / sunglasses – Repair kit.

19. Medical bag. *(No Liquids like eye drops, cough medicine, those go in 3-1-1 bag. Suggest cough drops, lip balm, band aids, pain relivers, aspirin, motion sickness tablets, upset stomach tablets.)*

20. Book. *(iPads and computers are great but power may become an issue. Get a paper copy, and get back to the good old paper book days.)* Do you know what they call people that do not bring something to read or do on an airplane? A **Nuisance.**

21. Compression socks *(helps with DVT -Deep Vein Thrombosis).*

22. Pen and writing pad *(good time to do "Thank You" cards, track your travels, or pen the next great novel).*

23. Non-electronic entertainment – Something to do.

24. Magazines. *(If you bring from home, remove the labels – your name and address. It was recommended by a friend and I do it now, tear out pages you want to read and take them with you, gives you something to read when electronics cannot be used, then discard - recycle.)*

25. Large scarf / shawl for ladies, light jacket for gentlemen.

26. Phone holder for rental car *(can go in checked luggage)*. A lot of states have hands free laws.

"You can get through life with bad manners, but it's easier with good manners."

~ Lillian Gish

Chapter 13: Prior To Boarding

1. **GO TO THE RESTROOM AND ALSO TAKE YOUR CHILDREN.**

2. Get something to eat *(before you get to airport or arrive early and enjoy a meal at the many restaurants at the airport, do not forget a gift card for that service person, if you want to make an impression invite them to have a meal with you)*, but do not take smelly, messy food on the aircraft. *(Stay away from peanuts – **Allergies**, garlic, onion, pizza, popcorn, burgers, tuna fish sandwich, etc. you get what items I'm referring too.)*

3. Get some snacks *(protein / granola bars, mints, candy, and a good Ziplock bag to keep them in)* and something to drink *(large bottle of water is great or carry your own bottle -- collapsible -- that can be filled after security, maybe at that nice restaurant where you are enjoying a meal before the flight).*

4. If you want a pillow or blanket, purchase one to carry. *(Replace the blanket with a good jacket.)*

5. Have your items out for easy accessibility during boarding *(tickets, passport).* Have other items in a

pouch, plastic bag that you can easily remove from your bag on plane, once in your seat *(book, headset, iPad)*.

6. Walk around, stretch, you are going to be sitting for a few hours.

7. One last item. **GO TO THE RESTROOM AND ALSO TAKE YOUR CHILDREN.**

"Be Kind whenever possible
It is Always Possible."

~ Dalai Lama

Chapter 14: Boarding

1. Do not use the airplane restroom during boarding, causes delays.

   GO TO THE RESTROOM AND ALSO TAKE YOUR CHILDREN WHILE IN WAITING AREA.

2. Have your documents ready *(paper tickets always good when your iPhone loses power, do not rely on Wi-Fi, have a copy).*

3. Do not crowd around the gate to board when you know they will board individuals that need assistance first, then first class / military in uniform, then by groups. *(A Group #6 on your ticket does not mean you are the 6th person to board it means you will be near the end. Check with the airline if you qualify for prior boarding assistance.)*

4. Do not be on your phone talking / texting while boarding, concentrate on getting to your seat.

5. Carrying your luggage is always an issue when boarding. You must be attentive and mindful of items you are carrying. Please walk with your items in front of you and close to the body.

6. Save the Over Head Storage Space over the **First Rows** of seats in each cabin (*first, business, and coach*) for individuals seated on the wall / bulkhead (*they have to put all their items there, they have NO storage space under seats like YOU DO*). Please, put your luggage in the compartment you are in, preferable above your seat.

Once you sit down, you should stay there, so make sure you have everything you will need for the flight once you settle in.

Reaching over other passengers to access the overhead storage during the flight is uncomfortable and unsafe for everyone.

"A warm smile is the universal language of Kindness."

~ William Arthur Ward

Chapter 15: At Your Seat

1. Try and step aside and let others pass.

2. Bag in overhead – place bag vertically *(wheels in, handle out)*, rather than horizontally in the bin. Only put **ONE** carry-on bag in the bin; the other one must fit in the open space under the seat in front of you *(except for passenger's seated in the first row of each cabin, this is the only storage space they receive).*

3. Offer to assist a fellow passenger in loading their bag *(flight attendants cannot lift bags into overhead bin).* Helps to make the boarding process more efficient for everyone else.

4. If you are in the aisle or middle seat, please step out to let other passengers into the row. *(Please do this if seat companions need to get up during the flight.)*

5. Items you need should be in the bag under the seat in front of you *(after you are seated is the time to retrieve them).*

6. Before you touch anything, clean it with sanitizing wipes. Wipe down your seat area, tray table, air vent, wall if seated by the window, window, window

shade, arm rest after you are seated, everything in the restroom before and after use.

7. Luggage should be placed in the storage area above your seat *(should not be accessed during flight)*. Anything you may need should be in bag under your seat.

8. If you need to store luggage over another row of seats, ask first. These passengers may have their bag down getting something and need the space. If you put your luggage in storage above another seat row, then you should not be getting anything out during flight. *(If you absolutely have to access during flight, then ask permission, you will be leaning in on the person in the aisle seat.)*

9. If your luggage has to be stored in a different class of service *(flight attendant must approve)* for the flight *(First, Business)*, then you do not go into that area / compartment during flight to get anything *(if it is absolutely necessary check with crew member first)*. **Never put your luggage in a separate compartment without crew member approval.**

10. Luggage stored behind your seat row for the flight. Then stay in your seat until all passengers have deplaned and then get up and retrieve your luggage.

*"Love and Kindness
Are Never Wasted
They Always
Make a Difference."*

~ Helen James

Chapter 16: On The Plane

1. Use your cell phone sparingly, why **NOT JUST TEXT.** *(We do not want to hear your business problems, family matters, or how important you think you are; calls if made should be brief, also that Bluetooth ear piece is not a fashion accessory.)*

2. Clean up after yourself *(everywhere, every time).*

3. Restroom *(wipe down your mess and clean out the sink, and always wear shoes).*

    GO TO THE RESTROOM AND ALSO TAKE YOUR CHILDREN BEFORE YOU BOARD.

    a. Fold your blanket and put it and your pillow on the seat when you get up *(First / Business class).*

    b. Do not put trash in the backseat magazine holder *(put it in the trash bag when flight attendant comes by, don't hand directly to them).*

    c. Straighten up the magazines in the back pocket.

    d. Straighten up your seatbelts when you get up
       to exit plane.

4. Your legs need to stay in your space, not in the aisle, or your seat companion area *(the width of the seat in front of you is your guide, and the only space your legs should be)*.

5. The seat belt **"ON"** light means **STAY IN YOUR SEAT.** You do not know everything the pilot does and there is a reason for it *(this is not your sign to go to the restroom)*.

6. First Class is for First Class, Business Class is for Business Class and Coach Class is for Coach Class. *(Stay in your compartment, if you want to use first / business class restrooms then pay for the privilege, like the passenger seated in those compartments have.)*

*"A **BAD ATTITUDE** is like a flat tire.*
You can't go anywhere until you
CHANGE IT."

~ Joyce Meyer

Chapter 17: The "DO's" On the Aircraft

1. Smile.

2. Be respectful, and mindful, especially of the space of those around you.

3. Respect the toilet. **Do not** take a lot of time, don't make a mess, and clean up after yourself.

   GO TO THE RESTROOM AND ALSO TAKE YOUR CHILDREN BEFORE YOU BOARD.

4. Be prepared.

5. Be patient.

6. Introduce yourself to your seat mates but do not be a chatterbox, *(if the person is reading a book, working on the computer, listening to music, trying to sleep)* be respectful.

"Be a little KINDER than you have to."

~ E. Bennett

Chapter 18: The "DO NOT's"

1. **Do Not** grab / jostle the back of the seat in front of you to get up. *(You interrupt that person's comfort and I may just put my chair back to give you less room).* Use the armrest. To better explain this; **DO NOT TOUCH ANY SEAT BUT YOURS.**

2. **Do Not** recline seats *(really, it is only a small amount and do you want someone doing it to you)*, without asking the person behind you *(that spilled drink on a computer could be costly).*

3. **Do Not** talk loudly or carry-on conversations with individuals, especially across an aisle *(I may find ways to annoy you later).*

4. **Do Not** put your tray table down and let your children pound on it.

5. **Do Not** kick or allow your children to kick the backs of seats.

   Note: Suggestion if a child is disturbing you. Kindness goes a long way.

   Turn toward the parent and smile.

   Ask about the child, a few pleasantries; age, never

flown much, does not like to be confined / cooped up, etc.

Then ask, could you maybe assist me with something. I am trying to get some work done and the little one is…*state issue, (hopefully the rapport you have established will help)*.

Remember the little gift bags I mentioned for children, these will help in this type situation.

6. **Do Not** ever ring the call button unless necessary *(it is not a play toy for children)*.

    a. Whatever your child does on a flight, *(or any public transport)* or crowded situation is not cute to the rest of us. That look I am or others are giving you should be saying something. *(Like, amusement would be stuffing him / her in the overhead compartment and smacking the day lights out of you until you learn manners. Did your parents let you get away with that? Just kidding, there should never be any violence, but we are thinking it.)*

7. **Do Not** put your feet:

    a. On the bulkhead / wall.

    b. Between the seat armrest.

    c. On seat in front of you.

    d. On windows.

    e. In the aisle.

    f. In other seat companion's area *(seat width in front of you is your guide and space).*

    g. On anything other than the floor.

8. **Do Not** crowd the toilet / galley area. **GO TO THE RESTROOM AND ALSO TAKE YOUR CHILDREN BEFORE YOU BOARD.**

9. **Do Not** floss or pick your teeth in the seat *(use the restroom).*

10. **Do Not** remove your shoes if you know you have an odor problem. *(Use a good foot powder even if you do not have a foot odor problem. Also be aware that on long flights your feet swell so wear comfortable shoes that are easy to put on / off. It is advisable to wear shoes and other clothing that has multiple uses.)*

11. **Do Not** move someone's items unless you ask. I may move your items after you go to sleep.

12. **Do Not** put items in the overhead that can break and if it is a coat or clothing put it on top of your luggage *(do not expect others to see it and not put their luggage on top of your items).*

13. **Do Not** fly, *SICK* at any time. Do you want to sit next to someone who is sneezing, coughing, or throwing up the entire flight?

14. **Do Not** consume a large amount of alcohol *(it dehydrates you).* If you sit next to a boozer and it becomes a problem in any way, contact the crew immediately.

*"Whoever one is,
and wherever one is,
one is always in the wrong
if one is rude."*

~ Maurice Baring

Chapter 19: DO NOT's for Flight Attendants

1. **Do Not** call Flight Attendants "Stewardess," this is no longer appropriate since attendants can be female or male. The correct wording is "ATTENDANT."

2. **Do Not** make fun of a name (like Candy or Honey).

3. **Do Not** ask to babysit *(ask a fellow passenger)*.

4. **Do Not** ask to give a massage (Really???).

5. **Do Not** argue.

6. **Do Not** ask for a date.

7. **Do Not,** ask for free mini bottles to take with you.

8. **Do Not** ask about meals *(what they offer is what they have. If they did not offer vegetarian, then they do not have it)*.

9. **Do Not** ask about delays.

10. **Do Not** ask about your next flight *(subscribe to flight following Apps)*.

"No matter how educated,
talented,
rich or cool you think you are,
how you treat people ultimately tells all.
Integrity is everything"

~ Author Unknown

Chapter 20: The Elephant in The Plane

"Center Seat Armrest"

1. Please allow the middle-seat passenger use of the armrests *(really, it is the proper resolution and least you can do for the person in the most uncomfortable seat, with limited seat space and leg room).*

   a. If you are seated next to a window you have an armrest and the wall to rest against.

   b. If you are seated on the aisle, you have an armrest and also the aisle to stretch your legs in when no one is walking by or service is in progress. *(If you stretch your legs in the aisle, then please stay awake, never impede on anyone's space.)*

2. Maintain your personal space.

3. Keep your legs within the width of the airplane seat in front of you.

"There can be no defense like elaborate courtesy."

~ E.V. Lucas

Chapter 21: Food / Beverage Service

1. When drink / food service begins, bring your seat back up *(I suggest never to recline your seat)* so the person behind you can enjoy their meal and not be cramped.

2. This is the time to stay in your seat and not crowd the aisle. It may take you a long time to get back to your seat *(remember, use the restroom before you board the aircraft)*.

3. When the food selection is given, choose from that. *(There are **NO** other options, a little research before your flight may let you know if there is going to be a meal or snack and if you can preorder.)*

4. Food service is when food is served, if this is an inconvenient time for you then live with it or do not eat.

5. Drink order, be specific what you want.

    a. If you order coffee / tea, tell them what you want in it *(cream, sugar, ice cubes, water)*. Do not make them ask several times or have to come back because you forgot to state what you needed when they were there.

b. If you order a cool drink, then state with / without ice *(I recommend no ice).*

"Manners are a sensitive awareness of the feelings of others.
If you have that awareness,
you have good manners,
no matter what fork you use."

~ Emily Post

Chapter 22: Getting Off the Plane

1. Politely and efficiently, everyone is eager to get off. Exit row-by-row.

2. Why do you stand up and crowd the aisle when the plane stops? Wait until others in front of you leave then you can get up and walk out. *(Standing up when plane stops, individual's temperature rise, it is crowed and congested, people trying to get bags, and **NOTHING MOVES FAST**. Try it.)*

3. You will have plenty of time to prepare to get off *(check you have everything)*.

4. If your luggage is behind the row you are seated in, then remain in your seat until everyone has deplaned.

"Politeness and consideration for others is like investing pennies and getting dollars back."

~ Thomas Sowell

A. C. T.
Action Changes Things

72

Chapter 23: Baggage Claim

1. Stay several feet back from the conveyor belt and do not approach until you see your baggage.

2. Bags look alike, check the one you took off the conveyor is yours *(get that special luggage strap with initials, see item list at end of book)*.

3. Use only approved porters if needed, **DO NOT** accept assistance from anyone that is not approved. *(Don't forget to Tip.)*

4. Some airports check your luggage stubs so be prepared.

5. Report lost luggage ASAP *(as soon as possible)*. Have a picture, size, and items inside *(make a picture before you leave)*. Do not delay in reporting / filing claims. Keep copies of receipts (clothing, personal items, etc.) related to unexpected expenses caused by airline loss *(possible refund on some expenses)*.

6. Check on lost luggage insurance with the credit card you used to book flight *(check before you go)*. *Know what your airlines covers and amounts.*

7. Look into additional travel insurance for trip /
    luggage.

*"Politeness is the art of choosing among
one's real thoughts."*

~ Abel Stevens

Chapter 24: First Aid / Save a Life

To better prepare you for medical emergencies **I suggest a local FIRST AID Course and to become certified in CPR *(yearly).*** Your knowledge in these areas could help save a life.

This First Aid area is to help you in certain situations, where medical personal may not be able to respond immediately.

This is <u>NO WAY</u> a medical guide.

The author of this book does not dispense medical advice or prescribe the use of any technique as a form of treatment for **Physical, Emotional or Medical Problems without the advice of a PHYSICIAN** either directly or indirectly.

Please take a course or research the different ways to handle emergency situations.

If <u>YOU</u> are handling the Emergency Situations;

* Notify another individual to Call Medical Assistance.

* Direct someone to go after Medical Kit / Defibrator.

* Get several people to get bystanders away from the area. It is already embarrassing for the individual in the situation.

* If in a large area direct someone to go outside to direct medical personnel.

* If performing CPR get others to be ready to assist, this is very demanding procedure.

Always call medical experts in any situations.

When traveling to another country put their emergency number (#) in your phone. *(Don't forget travel insurance – especially medical and especially for vacation packages, cruises, and international travel.)*

CALL 911 in U.S.

Check this website for emergency numbers in other countries before you go.

https://travel.state.gov/content/dam/students-abroad/pdfs/911_ABROAD.pdf

STROKE

TO HELP YOU RECOGNIZE THE SIGNS OF A POSSIBLE --- STROKE

Remember the acronym

F. A. S. T.

Face – Drooping

* ✳ Does one side of the face droop or is it numb.

* ✳ Ask the person to smile. Is the person's smile uneven?

Arm – Weakness

* ✳ Is one arm, weak or numb?

* ✳ Ask the person to raise both arms. Does one arm drift downward?

Speech – Difficulty

* ✳ Is speech slurred?

* ✳ Is the person unable to speak or hard to understand?

* ✳ Ask the person to repeat a simple sentence

like. "The sky is blue." Is the sentence repeated correctly?

Time – Call 9-1-1

* Immediately have someone call 911 if signs of symptoms, even if symptoms go away.

* Get the person to the hospital immediately.

* Record the time when the first symptoms appeared, medical team needs this *(the first hour is critical)*.

Beyond *F.A.S.T.* – *Other Symptoms You Should Know*

- Sudden **NUMBNESS** or weakness of face, arm, or leg, especially on one side of the body.

- Sudden **CONFUSION**, trouble speaking or understanding speech.

- Sudden **TROUBLE SEEING** in one or both eyes.

- Sudden **TROUBLE WALKING**, dizziness, loss of balance or coordination.

- Sudden **SEVERE HEADACHE** with no known cause.

If someone shows any of these symptoms, immediately call 9-1-1 or emergency medical services *(the first hour is critical)*.

POISON CONTROL

1 (800) 222-1222 (U.S.)

American Association of Poison Control Center's

Hours: 24 hours, 7 days a week

Languages: English

Website: www.aapcc.org

BLEEDING

P. E. E. P.

Position – the person on flat surface if possible

Expose – the injury

Elevate *(raise)* – the wound

Pressure – apply to the area

Immediately call 9-1-1 or Emergency Medical Services

SHOCK

Always be aware that shock may overcome any person at any time for any situation.

Some simple guidelines for **SHOCK**

Face is **RED**, raise the **HEAD**

Face is **PALE**, raise the **TAIL**

Immediately call 9-1-1 or Emergency Medical Services

HEART ATTACK

WARNING SIGNS

P. U. L. S. E.

Persistent – Chest Pain

Upset – Stomach

Light – Headedness *(Dizzy)*

Shortness – Breath

Excessive – Sweating

Immediately call 9-1-1 or Emergency Medical Services

Heimlich (choking)

Ask the victim if they are choking; the person will usually not be able to talk.

* Stand behind the victim,

* Wrap your arms around them,

* Place a fist between the person's ribcage and belly button,

* Place your other hand over the fist,

* Deliver up to five (5) thrust upward,

* Keep doing this until the foreign object is dislodged.

* This technique is only for adults.

Immediately call 9-1-1 or Emergency Medical Services

CPR (Cardiopulmonary Resuscitation)

Immediately call 9-1-1 or Emergency Medical Services

Performed to provide chest compressions and rescue breaths *(American Heart Association does not mandate that everyone learn rescue breathing but keep doing compressions.)* **Most important is to continue compressions if you do not want to do the Breaths.**

* **Adult – 100/120 compressions per minute about 2-3 inches (5-6cm) deep**

* **Breaths – after 30 compressions, tilt head back, chin up. Pinch nose, give 2-3 breaths. Most important is to continue compressions if you do not want to do the breaths.**

CPR - Child and Infant

* **Gently deliver quick compressions that are about 1.5 inches (3-4 cm) deep.**

Chapter 25: Suggested Travel Items

Search Amazon and other sites for items that may match your needs.

When traveling please check with your mode of travel Company *(Airline, Cruise Ships, Train, Bus, etc.)* on what is allowable for carry on and checked baggage. Know the rules for any Country, Providence, State, Territory you are traveling in.

When visiting a product page on Amazon look under the area on the product description. You will see an area labeled something like **Visit the (name Product) Store**. Here you will find other products that might be of benefit to you

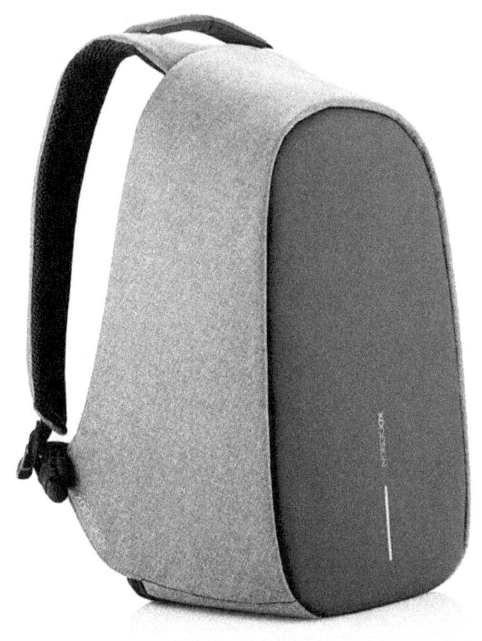

XD Design Bobby Pro Anti-Theft Backpack USB/Type C (Unisex Bag)

Product Dimensions: 12.4 x 4.9 x 18.1 inches

(Great No outside pockets for people to get into)

https://www.amazon.com/Design-Anti-Theft-Laptop-Backpack-Unisex/dp/B079VP1BLR/ref=sr_1_6?crid=OP57A93F1UKS&dchild=1&keywords=xdesign+backpack&qid=1633484462&sprefix=ex+design+back%-2Caps%2C187&sr=8-6

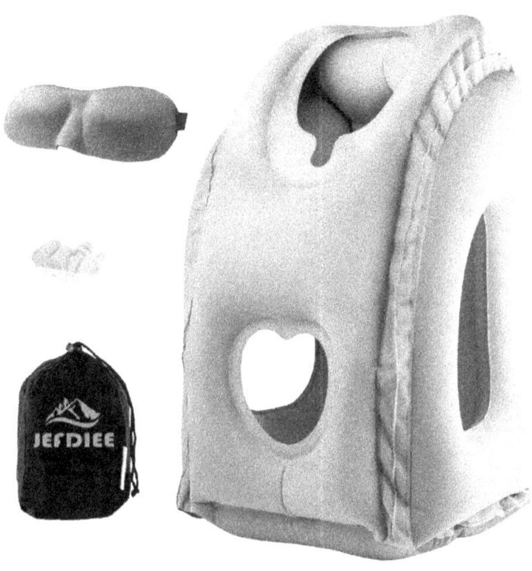

JefDiee Inflatable Travel Pillow, Airplane Neck Pillow Comfortably Supports Head and Chin for Airplanes, Trains, Cars and Office Napping with 3D Eye Mask

(That Beach Ball I mentioned can replace this.)

https://www.amazon.com/Inflatable-Airplane-Comfortably-Airplanes-Drawstring/dp/B083NVHN13/ref=sr_1_2_sspa?crid=31QFKAQS3ORAA&dchild=1&keywords=jefdiee+inflatable+travel+pillow&qid=1632354885&smid=A-4OD2PIPZGM4U&sprefix=jefdiee+inflatable+pillow%2C-aps%2C191&sr=8-2-spons&psc=1&spLa=ZW5jcnl-wdGVkUXVhbGlmaWVyPUEyRkZKWExSRFdGTkFR-JmVuY3J5cHRlZElkPUEwMjUyNDk0MUUxNzUUTFNK-TVFGRCZlbmNyeXB0ZWRBZElkPUEwMTU1NDM-5MTg1SDY1MVBYQzlLRCZ3aWRnZXROYW1lPXNwX-2F0ZiZhY3Rpb249Y2xpY2tSZWRpcmVjdCZkb05vdEx-vZ0NsaWNrPXRydWU=

Jefdiee Inflatable Foot Pillow

I recommend this only for long flights

Amazon.com: JefDiee Inflatable Travel Foot Rest Pillow, Kids Airplane Bed, Adjustable 3 Layers Height Leg Rest Pillow, Adults Travel Essentials Great for Airplane, Office, Home, Trains, Cars : Home & Kitchen

NEW Travelrest i-Lene Travel Pillow - The Best Neck Pillows for Airplanes - Attaches to Airplane Headrest - Dual-Density Memory Foam - Plush Washable Removable Cover (2-Year Warranty)

https://www.amazon.com/Travelrest-All-Ultimate-Travel-Pillow/dp/B01GQVGS98/ref=sr_1_7?crid=2R3JG44VZA79P&dchild=1&keywords=travelrest+ultimate+travel+pillow+%26+neck+pillow&qid=1633485974&sprefix=travelrest%2Caps%2C181&sr=8-7

BubbleBum Inflatable Backless Booster Car Seat, Black

https://www.amazon.com/BubbleBum-Backless-Inflatable-Booster-Black/dp/B00AQYZCXK/ref=sr_1_2?dchild=1&keywords=inflatable+car+seat&qid=1587259075&s=baby-products&sr=1-2

Smoke Escape Hood

www.firstaidglobal.com

Stall Mates Wipes: Flushable, individually wrapped wipes for travel. Unscented with Vitamin-E & Aloe, 100% Biodegradable (30 on-the-go singles)

https://stallmateswipes.com/

Mission Darkness Non-Window Faraday Bag for Tablets - Device Shielding for Law Enforcement, Military, Executive Privacy, EMP Protection, Travel & Data Security, Anti-Hacking & Anti-Tracking Assurance

https://www.amazon.com/s?k=Mission+Darkness+Non-Window+Faraday+Bag+for+Tablets+-+Device+Shielding+for+Law+Enforcement%2C+Military%2C+Executive+Privacy%2C+EMP+Protection%2C+Travel+%26+Data+Security%2C+Anti-Hacking+%26+Anti-Tracking+Assurance&ref=nb_sb_noss

Reliance Safego, Indoor/Outside Portable Security, Black, Different color's available

https://www.amazon.com/s?k=SAFEGO+-Portable+Indoor%2FOutdoor+Lock+Box-+Safe+with+Key+and+Combination+Access+%28Compact%2C+Black%29&ref=nb_sb_noss

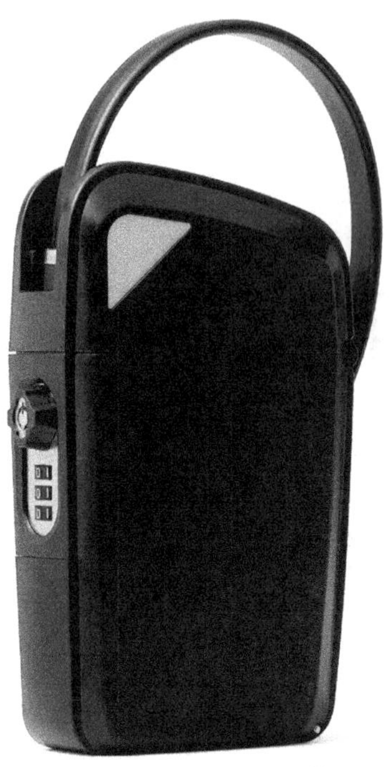

SAFEGO Portable Indoor/Outdoor Lock Box Safe with Key and Combination Access (Compact)

https://www.amazon.com/s?k=SAFEGO+Portable+Indoor%2FOutdoor+Lock+Box+Safe+with+Key+and+Combination+Access+%28Compact%2C+Black%29&ref=nb_sb_noss

Fire Escape Mask

www.firemask.com

Readers please use code: CONN15 for a discount

https://firemask.com/collections/frontpage/products/
firemask-f-60-fume-gas-and-smoke-mask-with-hood-for-
fire-safety-in-tall-buildings-hospitals-schools-retirement-
homes-emergency-vehicles-breath-easily-for-60-minutes-
even-in-heavy-smoke-made-for-children-and-adults

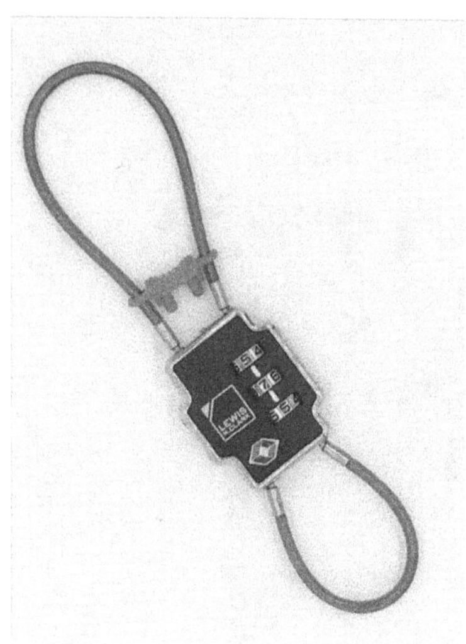 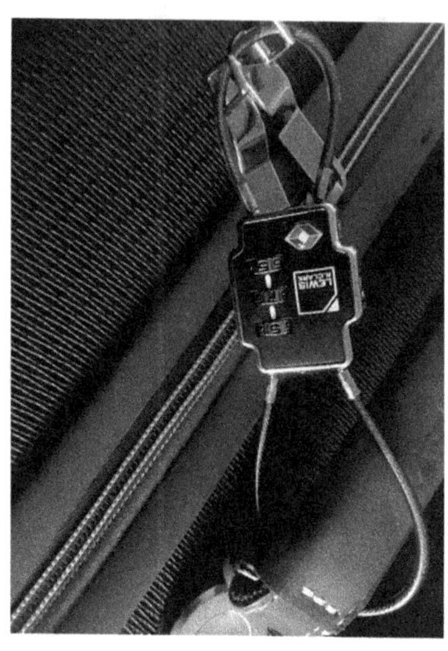

Lewis N Clark Triple Security Lock: TSA Luggage Locks for Suitcases, Carry On, Laptop Bag & More, Set Combination Lock to Create Secure Padlock for Travel, Vacation, Business, or Backpacking

(Locks zippers to handle so it can't be opened)

ZzzBand Airline Pilot Created Travel Pillow Alternative -The Necks Best Thing to First Class – Patented *(Straps to Headrest)*

https://www.amazon.com/ZzzBand-Created-Travel-Alternative-Patented/dp/B016U6WVTA/ref=sr_1_93?dchild=1&keywords=zzz+travel+pillow&qid=1633486117&sr=8-93

PCS Luggage Straps Suitcase Belt, ZINZ High Elastic Heavy Duty Bag Straps Bungees Travel Accessories Adjustable. With name or initials embroidered.
(Use initials or nickname, not full name)

https://www.amazon.com/Personalized-Embroidered-Luggage-Approved-Straps/dp/B0797HZ1T7/ref=sr_1_5?dchild=1&keywords=weavers+luggage+strap&qid=1633485559&sr=8-5

Initial Luggage Tag with Full Privacy Cover and Stainless-Steel Loop (Black, with your Initial)
(Use last name and phone number of your office, or family member, NO BUSINESS CARD)

https://www.amazon.com/Initial-Luggage-Privacy-Cover-Stainless/dp/B06WW1CJKR/ref=sr_1_3?crid=1N5KRIDLEIO59&dchild=1&keywords=shacke+luggage+tag+initial&qid=1633485722&sprefix=Shacke+Luggage+tag%2Caps%2C209&sr=8-3

Portable Travel Blanket Airplane Office 4 in 1 Micro Mink Fleece Poncho Blanket, Pocket and Built-in Bag - Great for Airplane, Car, Train, Ultra Soft and Cozy, Grey

(I only suggest this for long flights)

https://www.amazon.com/Portable-Travel-Blanket-Airplane-Folable/dp/B07TRQBTF4/ref=sr_1_40?dchild=1&keywords=travel+blanket&qid=1633486473&sr=8-40

Power Strip Non-Surge Protector, with 3 USB Ports, 3 Outlets, 5ft Heavy Duty Braided Extension Cord, Wall Mount, Flat Plug, Multi Outlet Extender

https://www.amazon.com/Desktop-Charging-Protector-Extension-Christmas/dp/B07TW5FVVP/ref=sr_1_4?dchild=1&keywords=Power+Strip+Non-Surge+Protector%2C+with+3+USB+Ports%2C+3+Outlets%2C+5ft+Heavy+Duty+Braided+Extension+-Cord%2C+Wall+Mount%2C+Flat+Plug%2C+-Multi+Outlet+Extender&qid=1635978719&qsid=136-4126306-2717641&sr=8-4&sres=B-096DGLVBH%2CB092J8LPWR%2CB08YY9X-1JV%2CB07TW5FVVP%2CB099NFLB64%2CB07V32P-J59%2CB07ZRDGF6Y%2CB08CTHF7JZ%2CB082D-VCCDR%2CB07WQS9V2G%2CB07F2L48F8%2C-B07GZNHVT4%2CB07B5RK8C7%2CB01K73M-8VS%2CB083S6WTPX%2CB07JG6N25Z&srpt=POWER_STRIP

Everlasting Comfort Airplane Footrest - Ergonomic Adjustable Foot and Heel Hammock - Memory Foam Portable Air Plane Flying Travel Foot Rest - Long Airplane Flight Accessories for Feet (Black)

(If you use this remember not to joggle seat you attach to.)

https://www.amazon.com/Foot-Rest-Airplane-Footrest-Hammock/dp/B086TXRD3C/ref=sr_1_1_sspa?dchild=1&keywords=Airplane+Foot+Hammock+%28Memory+Foam%29%2C+Perfect+Airplane+Footrest+to+Relax+Your+Feet%7CFoot+Hammock+for+Airplane+Travel+Accessories%2C+Desk+Foot+Hammock%2C+Travel+Foot+Rest%2C+Comfy+Foot+Hanger+Airplane&qid=1635979208&sr=8-1-spons&psc=1&spLa=ZW5jcnlwdGVkUXVhbGlmaWVyPUFGOUlKU05TVzY5RUkmZW5jcnlwdGVkSWQ9QTA2NzIwNzkxSzZEQzJCCVDZSQVY1JmVuY3J5cHRlZEFkSWQ9QTA2NDA1MzgzTlFCTFRHSllNNTM0JndpZGdldE5hbWU9c3BfYXRmJmFjdGlvbj1jbGlja1JlZGlyZWN0JmRvTm90TG9nQ2xpY2s9dHJ1ZQ==

Solar Power Bank 30000mAh, Solar Charger, Qi Wireless Charger, Outputs 5V/3A High-Speed & 2 Inputs Huge Capacity Phone Charger for Smartphones

https://www.amazon.com/Chargers-Dualpow-Porta-ble-Flashlight-Smartphones/dp/B082481YQ8/ref=s-r_1_64?dchild=1&keywords=lifepod&qid=1635978579&sr=8-64

Portable Charger 30000mah, Baseus USB C PD 3.0 Fast Charging 65W Power Bank, 5-outport LED Display Battery Pack for MacBook Pro, Dell XPS, iPhone 12 Mini Pro Max, iPad Pro, Galaxy S20, Switch and More

https://www.amazon.com/30000mah-Baseus-Portable-Charger-Charging/dp/B08JV4W4NY/ref=sr_1_3?d-child=1&keywords=Portable+Charger+30000mah%2C+-Baseus+USB+C+PD+3.0&qid=1633745404&sr=8-3

Baseus 8-in-1 USB C Hub Docking Station, USB C Adapter with 4K HDMI, 3 USB 3.0, TF/SD Reader, Ethernet, 100W Power Delivery for MacBook Pro, Surface Pro,...

https://www.amazon.com/Baseus-Docking-Station-Ethernet-Delivery/dp/B08X-73SVXN/ref=sr_1_2_sspa?dchild=1&keywords=Baseus+8-in-1+USB&qid=1633745297&sr=8-2-spons&psc=1&smid=A33IAQUVRW6L-GA&spLa=ZW5jcnlwdGVkUXVhbGlmaWVyPUF-BOVNRTVlBWUhKRjkmZW5jcnlwdGVkSWQ9QTAz-NTc3MDczVUNPSkVYQjk5VUIwJmVuY3J5cHRlZE-FkSWQ9QTA3MzE4MzgzT1VQQlA3UzhPV0Emd2lkZ-2V0TmFtZT1zcF9hdGYmYWN0aW9uPWNsaWNrUm-VkaXJlY3QmZG9Ob3RMb2dDbGljaz10cnVl

International Travel Plug Adapter, TESSAN Universal Power Adaptor with 4 USB Outlets, Worldwide All in One Wall Charger Converter for China USA EU Europe UK Thailand Japan Australia (Type G/C/A/I)

https://www.amazon.com/Universal-Adapter-TES-SAN-International-Adaptor/dp/B083SBDMHM/ref=s-r_1_5?dchild=1&keywords=International+Travel+Plug+-Adapter%2C+TESSAN&qid=1633745678&sr=8-5

USB C Charger, Baseus 100W 4-Port GaN II Charging Station, Fast USB C Charger Block for iPhone 12/12 Pro/12 Pro Max/SE/11/XR/XS, Samsung, MacBook Pro/Air, iPad, Laptops, AirPods, Apple Watch, Black

https://www.amazon.com/Charger-Baseus-Charging-Station-Samsung/dp/B097XRTQHY/ref=sr_1_1_sspa?dchild=1&keywords=USB+C+Charger%2C+Baseus+100W+4-Port+GaN+II+Charging+Station&qid=1633745577&sr=8-1-spons&psc=1&spLa=ZW5jcnlwdGVkUXVhbGlmaWVyPUExWUNFOFFYNEdLUkRWJmVuY3J5cHRlZElkPUEwMjU2OTAzMk1aRFM4RUlQQ0RLRSZlbmNyeXB0ZWRBZElkPUEwMzc2MzYyMVJVNDdPRVk5U0xxWUyZ3aWRnZXROYW1lPXNwX2F0ZiZhY3Rpb249Y2xpY2tSZWRpcmVjdCZkb05vdEExvZ0NsaWNrPXRydWU=

Travel Power Strip with USB - NTONPOWER 2 Outlets 3 USB Portable Desktop Charging Station, 15 inches Wrapped Short Extension Cord for Hotels, Cruise, Nightstand, Airports, Conference Room – Black

https://www.amazon.com/NTONPOWER-Outlets-Extension-Nightstand-Conference/dp/B072N854DK/ref=sr_1_50?dchild=1&keywords=BESTTEN%2B-Travel%2BPower%2BStrip%2BSurge%2BProtector%2C%2B2.4A%2BDual%2BUSB%2B-Charging%2BPorts%2Band%2B3%2BOutlets%-2C%2B300%2BJoules%2C%2B18in%2BExtension%2B-Cord%2C%2BETL%2BCertified%2C%2BBlack&qid=1633746310&sr=8-50&th=1

Ziploc Space Bags, Travel Bag for Suitcase, Organization

https://www.amazon.com/Space-Roll-up-Travel-Carry-Suitcase/dp/B00JM9AIGG/ref=sr_1_2?crid=2ST-PHZIC5C0P&dchild=1&keywords=ziploc+space+bags+-suitcase+travel&qid=1633748713&sprefix=Ziploc+Space+Bags%2C+Travel+Bag+for+Suitcase%-2Caps%2C227&sr=8-2

Pure Zen Tea Tumbler with Infuser - BPA Free Double Wall Glass Travel Tea Mug with Stainless Steel Filter - Leakproof Tea Bottle with Strainer for Loose Leaf Tea and Fruit Water 13 Ounce

*(I love this for brewing my own tea or coffee. I order my tea from **www.sterlingtea.com**.)*

https://www.amazon.com/Pure-Zen-Tea-Stainless-Leakproof/dp/B01MA1WWQN/ref=sr_1_1?dchild=1&keywords=Pure+Zen+Tea+Tumbler+with+Infuser&qid=1587259153&s=baby-products&sr=8-1

BESTEK 300W Power Inverter for Car, Inverter DC 12V to 110V AC Converter Car Outlet Adapter with USB-C PD Cigarette Lighter Plug, 2 AC Charger Outlets and Dual 2.4A USB Ports Total 4.8A Output, **Red**

https://www.amazon.com/BESTEK-Inverter-Converter-Adapter-Cigarette/dp/B08MJ6ZK4H/ref=sr_1_1?dchild=1&keywords=BESTEK+300W+Power+Inverter+-for+Car%2C+Inverter+DC+12V+to+110V+AC+Converter+Car+Outlet+Adapter+with+USB-C+PD+Cigarette+Lighter+Plug%2C+2+AC+Charger+Outlets+and+Dual+2.4A+USB+Ports+Total+4.8A+Output%2C+Red&qid=1633814337&sr=8-1

Rechargeable Book Light, Merisky LED Clip on Reading Light for Book in Bed, 3 Color × 3 Brightness, Up to 60 Hours Eye Care Reading, Warm & White, Perfect for Kids, Bed Headboard & Travel

(If you are going to read, or use a computer, get one, do not use the overhead light)

LifeStraw Personal Water Filter

https://www.amazon.com/s?k=LifeStraw+Personal+Water+Filter&ref=nb_sb_noss_2

Car Charger Fast Charge Adapter, SOMOSTEL Auto Seat Belt Cutter Window Breaker Power Bank Crash Safe Emergency Escape Tool Red Beacon Flashlight Compatible with Samsung Galaxy S9 S8, LG G7 V20 Stylo 4

https://www.amazon.com/Charger-SOMOSTEL-Emergency-Flashlight-Compatible/dp/B075F5G97T/ref=sr_1_1?dchild=1&keywords=Car+Charger+-Fast+Charge+Adapter%2C+SOMOSTEL+Auto+Seat+-Belt+Cutter+Window&qid=1633481795&sr=8-1

Mace Brand Dorm Room Essential Security Kit – Includes Brand Night Defender Pepper Gel with LED Light, Personal Alarm That Emits 130dB, and a Stun Gun – Batteries Included, Great for Self-Defense

https://www.amazon.com/Mace-Brand-Essentials-Security-Black/dp/B08VJJGGX1/ref=sr_1_1?dchild=1&keywords=mace%2B-Brand%2BDorm%2BRoom%2BEssential%2BSecurity-ty%2BKit%2B%E2%80%93%2BIncludes%2BBrand%2B-Night%2BDefender%2BPepper%2BGel%2B-with%2BLED%2BLight%2C%2BPersonal%2BAlarm%2B-That%2BEmits%2B130dB%2C%2Band%2Ba%2B-Stun%2BGun%2B%E2%80%93%2BBatter-ies%2BIncluded%2C%2BGreat%2Bfor%2BSelf-De-fense&qid=1633813805&sr=8-1&th=1

AUKEY Car Phone Mount Air Vent Cell Phone Holder for Car Compatible with iPhone 11/11 Pro/Xs/XS Max / 8/7 / 6, Google Pixel 3 XL, Samsung Galaxy S9+, and Other Phones

https://www.amazon.com/s?k=AUKEY+Car+-Phone+Mount+Air+Vent+Cell+Phone+Holder+for+-Car+Compatible+with+iPhone+11%2F11+Pro%2FX-s%2FXS+Max+%2F+8%2F7+%2F+6%2C+Google+Pixel-+3+XL%2C+Samsung+Galaxy+S9%2B%2C+and+Other+-Phones&ref=nb_sb_noss

Beilite Wedding Dress Garment Bag Dust Cover Storage Travel Bag

https://www.amazon.com/Beilite-Wedding-Garment-Stor-age-Travel/dp/B01GFCRFMW/ref=sr_1_1?dchild=1&key-words=Beilite+Wedding+Dress+Garment+Bag+Dust+-Cover+Storage+Travel+Bag&qid=1635982295&qs id=136-4126306-2717641&sr=8-1&sres=B01GFCRFM-W%2CB088LV8RLD%2CB07DJ2XJ4W%2CB0852XM-2KC%2CB07K9MPWFF%2CB08DNGP5P5%2CB083W-G212T%2CB0056DHZ6S%2CB07JF8N39B%2C-B01LA746D8%2CB00E7V8BZ4%2CB007RE9V0M%2CB-00TR60LB6%2CB01NCEELHW%2CB007629XJE%2CB-01N5QBUUT%2CB07CTBCM84%2CB01MF9DJC-G%2CB07KQ6XTGV%2CB010P3AODY

Chapter 26: Airline Info

Aeroflot
https://www.aeroflot.com/us-en

Aerolineas (Argentina)
https://www.aerolineas.com.ar/

Aeromexico
https://www.aeromexico.com/en-us

Alaska Airlines
https://www.alaskaair.com/

Alitalia
https://www.alitalia.com/en_us/

All Nippon Airways
https://www.ana.co.jp/

Allegiant Air
https://www.allegiantair.com/home

American Airlines
https://www.aa.com/homePage.do
800.433.7300

Asiana Airline
https://flyasiana.com/C/US/EN/index

Atlas Air
  https://www.atlasair.com/

Austrian Airlines
  https://www.austrian.com/

Avianca
  https://www.avianca.com/us/en/

Bahamas Air
  http://www.bahamasair.com/

Bangkok Airways
  https://www.bangkokair.com/

Baltic Airlines
  https://www.airbaltic.com/

British Airways
  https://www.britishairways.com/

Botswana Air
  https://www.airbotswana.co.bw/

Bulgaria Air
  https://www.air.bg/en/

Canada Air
  https://www.aircanada.com/ca/en/aco/home.html

Cape Air
  https://www.capeair.com/

Cathay Pacific Airways
  https://www.cathaypacific.com/

Cayman Airways
https://www.caymanairways.com/

China Airways
https://www.china-airlines.com/us/en

China Eastern Airlines
https://us.ceair.com/en/

China Southern
https://www.csair.com/en/

Comair
https://www.comair.co.za/

Continental Airlines
https://www.united.com/en/us

Copa Airlines
https://www.copaair.com/en/web/us

Croatia Airlines
https://www.croatiaairlines.com/

Cyprus Airways
https://www.cyprusairways.com/

Czech Airlines
https://www.csa.cz/cz-en/

Delta Airlines
https://www.delta.com/

DHL WorldWide
https://www.dhl.com/en/express.html

East African Safari Air
  https://www.yatra.com

Easy Jet Airlines
  https://www.easyjet.com/en/

Egypt Air
  https://www.egyptair.com/

EL AL Israel Airlines
  https://www.elal.com/

Emirates Air
  https://www.emirates.com/

Ethiopian Airlines
  https://www.ethiopianairlines.com/aa

Europa Air
  https://www.aireuropa.com/

EVA Airways
  https://www.evaair.com/en-us/

Fiji Air
  https://www.fijiairways.com/

Finnair
  https://www.finnair.com/

France Air
  https://www.airfrance.com

Frontier
  https://www.flyfrontier.com/

Garuda Indonesia
  https://www.garuda-indonesia.com/

Gulf Air
  https://www.gulfair.com/

Hawaiian Airlines
  https://www.hawaiianairlines.com/

Iberia
  https://www.iberia.com/us/

Icelandair
  https://www.icelandair.com/

India Air
  http://www.airindia.com/

Island Air
  https://www.islandairx.com/

Jamaica Air
  http://ww38.airjamaica.com

Japan Airlines
  https://www.jal.co.jp/jp/en/

JetBlue Airlines
  https://www.jetblue.com/

Kenmore Air
  https://www.kenmoreair.com/

Kenya Air
  https://www.airkenya.com/

Kenya Airways
  https://www.kenya-airways.com/us/en/

KLM Airlines
  https://www.klm.com/home/us/en
  1 (800) 618-0104

Korean Air
  https://www.koreanair.com/global/en.html
  1 (800) 438-5000

Kulula Airlines
  https://www.kulula.com/

Kuwait Airways
  https://kuwaitairways.com/en
  1-800-458-9248

Lacsa Costa Rica
  https://www.alternativeairlines.com/lacsa-airlines

LATAM LanChile Air
  https://www.latam.com/en_us/
  1 (866) 435-9526

Lauda Airlines
  https://www.laudamotion.com/la/de/

LOT Polish Airlines
  https://www.lot.com/us/en/
  1 (212) 789-0970

Lufthansa
  https://www.lufthansa.com/us/en/homepage
  1 (800) 645-3880

Madagascar Air
   https://www.airmadagascar.com/fr

Malta Air
   https://www.airmalta.com/

Malaysia Airlines
   https://www.malaysiaairlines.com/us/en.html
   1 (800) 552-9264

Mauritius Air
   https://www.airmauritius.com/

Mesa Airlines
   http://www.mesa-air.com/

MIAT Mongolian Air
   https://www.miat.com/

Middle East MEA Air
   https://www.mea.com.lb/

Moldova Air
   http://www.airindia.com/

Nantucket Airlines
   https://www.nantucketairlines.com/

New England Airlines
   http://blockislandsairline.com/

New Zealand Air
   https://www.airnewzealand.com/iah

Norwegian Air Shuttle
   https://www.norwegian.com/en/

Olympic Airways
https://www.olympicair.com/en/

Pacific Coastal Airlines
https://www.pacificcoastal.com/

Pelita Air Services
https://www.pelita-air.com/

Philippine Airlines
https://www.philippineairlines.com/en

Portugal Air
https://www.flytap.com/

PIA Pakistan Airlines
https://www.piac.com.pk/

Qantas Airways
https://www.qantas.com/us/en.html
1 (800) 227-4500

Royal Air Maroc
https://www.royalairmaroc.com/us-en

Royal Jordanian Airlines
https://rj.com/

Royal Nepal
https://www.nepalairlines.com.np/home

Ryanair
https://www.ryanair.com/us/en

SAS Scandinavian Air
https://www.flysas.com/en/
1 (800) 221-2350

Saudia Arabian Airlines
https://www.saudia.com/

Scenic Airlines
https://www.scenic.com/ (Grand Canyon)

Singapore Airlines
https://www.singaporeair.com/en

SN Brussels Airlines
https://www.brusselsairlines.com/

Solomon Airlines
https://www.flysolomons.com/

South African Airways
https://www.flysaa.com/en

Southwest Airlines
https://www.southwest.com/
1.800.I.FLY.SWA

Spirit Airlines
https://www.spirit.com/

Sir Lankan Air
https://www.srilankan.com/en_uk/us

Sun Country Airlines
https://www.suncountry.com/

Sunshine Air
https://www.airsunshine.com/

Suriname Airways
https://www.flyslm.com/en/

SWISS Air
https://www.swiss.com/ch/en
1 (877) 359-7947

TAP Air Portugal
https://www.flytap.com/
1 (800) 221-7370

TAME (Galapagos)
https://www.tame.com.ec/index.php/en/

Tahiti Nui Air
https://www.airtahitinui.com/us-en

Transat Air
https://www.airtransat.com

Zimbabwe Air
http://ww43.airzimbabwe.com/

Chapter 27: Checklist

Items for Travel

Suitcase	
Carry-on Bag / Backpack	
TSA Luggage Lock – Figure 8 Style *(secures zippers to handle)*	
Luggage Tag w / Initial *(secures name inside)*	
Blanket	
Compressions Socks	
Eye Mask	
Ear Plugs / Noise Cancelling Headset	
Power Cord / Strip	
Solar Portable Power Bank	
USB Hub	
Smoke Mask / Hood	
Sanitize Wipes / Gel	
Sunblock / Lotion	
Rain Poncho	
Car Phone Holder *(for checked luggage)*	
Glow Sticks *(for Checked Luggage)*	
Ziploc Travel Bags	

Tea Tumbler / Water Bottle	
Rechargeable Book Light	
Portable Travel Safe	
Personal Alarm	

Your Packing Checklist *(Carry-On)*

Item	Packed	Packed

Your Packing Checklist *(Checked)*

Item	Packed	Packed

The First Aid cards below are for you to photo and have on your phone or copy, cut and laminate to carry in your wallet, purse, consider an additional set for your vehicles.

<u>STROKE</u> - *acronym F.A.S.T.*

Face – **Drooping**
- Does one side of the face droop or is it numb
- Ask the person to smile, Is SMILE uneven

Arm – **Weakness**
- Is one arm weak or numb
- Ask the person to raise arms. Does one arm drift down

Speech – **Difficulty**
- Is speech Slurred
- Is person unable to speak or hard to understand
- Ask person to repeat a simple sentence like, "The Sky is Blue"

Time – **Call 9-1-1 or Emergency Medical Services**

<u>POISON CONTROL</u>

1 (800) 222-1222 (U.S.)

***American Association of
Poison Control Centers***

Hours: 24 hours, 7 days a week
Languages: English
Website: www.aapcc.org

<u>**SHOCK**</u>

Always be aware that shock may overcome any person at any time for any situation.

Simple guidelines for **SHOCK**
Face is **RED**, raise the **HEAD**
Face is **PALE**, raise the **TAIL**

Call 9-1-1 or Emergency Medical Services

<u>BLEEDING</u> – acronym **P.E.E.P.**

Position – person on flat surface
Expose – the Injury
Elevate (raise) – the wound
Pressure – apply to the area

**Call 9-1-1 or
Emergency Medical Services**

<u>**Heart Attack**</u> *Warning Signs*

Persistent – Chest Pain
Upset – Stomach
Light – Headedness (Dizzy)
Shortness – Breath
Excessive – Sweating

**Call 9-1-1 or
Emergency Medical Services**

CPR – ADULT

Adult – 100/120 compressions per minute about 2-3 inches (5-6cm) deep

Breaths – after 30 compressions, tilt head back, chin up. Pinch nose, give 2-3 breaths

Most important is to continue compressions if you don't want to do breaths

CPR – Child / Infant

Gently deliver quick compressions about 1.5 inches (3-4cm) deep

Tilt the head of the child/infant and gently provide two (2) rescue breaths

Continue CPR until emergency response team is ready to take over

Heimlich (chocking)
For ADULTS ONLY

Ask person if they are chocking; the person will usually not be able to talk

Stand behind the victim

Wrap your arms around them

Place a fist between the person's ribcage and belly button

Place your other hand over the fist

Deliver up to five (5) thrust upward

Keep doing this until the foreign object is dislodged

**Call 9-1-1 or
Emergency Medical Services**

Connect with Michael

If you would like to have Michael as a Speaker, Trainer or Consultant he can be reached at:

Email – mdlspeaks@outlook.com

LinkedIn - linkedin.com/in/mikelynnspeaks

Michael specializes in numerous topics and subject areas related to:

> Protocol
> Etiquette
> Travel / Home / Personal Security
> Exhibitions / Trade Shows

Michael customizes all presentations to meet your needs. Don't see a presentation that suits your needs? Contact us and we can work with you to put together a program that fits.

Each course comes with PowerPoint Presentation, Attendee Handout, Course Description & LOEs (*Learning Outcome Essentials*), Test

If this book has been beneficial and interesting, please leave a review on Amazon

I hope this book has brought attention to certain areas of Travel Etiquette, especially at airports and on airplanes.

Please share any of your adventures or pictures with me.

Please help get CIVILITY back into travel

About the Author

Michael Lynn, CEM, CME, CMM, CMP, CPC, CPECP, is a Co-founding Partner of Global Protocol, Etiquette & Civility Academy.

Mike is retired Director Exhibitions, Events, and Protocol for a major U.S. Defense Company where he was responsible for the development and coordination of worldwide trade / exhibitions, special events, meetings, conventions, and VIP / protocol functions. Mike has over 30 years of industry experience and contributes strong talent, long-range strategic planning, and onsite tactical coordination to any project.

Mike received dual Master's degrees from Embry Riddle University of Florida in Management and Science. Mike earned his Bachelor's degree in Aeronautics from Embry Riddle University. He has degrees in Flight Engineering and Aircraft Maintenance from the United States Air Force.

Known as "The Ambassador of Certifications," he currently holds Exhibition, Event and Protocol accreditations as a: CEM, CME, CMM, CMP, CPC, CPECP. Mike has held positions in over 12 professional and community associations and has served on the E2MA, IAEE, TSEA, CMP, and Hero Portraits Board of Directors and as Chair – International Center Exhibition & Event Marketing (ICEEM) board. Mike is a member of and serves on the education committee of the Protocol Diplomacy International – Protocol Officers Association (PDI-POA). He has served on the Exhibition Industry Task Force (EITF), Accepted Practices Exchange (APEX) Contracts Committee, the Travel Industry Advocacy Committee, and was a member of Meeting Professionals International (MPI).

Mike's is retired from the United States Air Force where his distinguished military career was highlighted when honored to serve ten years in the 89th Special Air Mission (SAM) unit, flying the U.S. President, Vice President, Cabinet and Foreign Leaders.

Mike has qualified on the VC-118A, C-47, T-29, C-141A/B, VC-137B/C, B-727, and B747 aircraft, with over 12,000 hour's flight time as a Flight Engineer, Instructor, and Examiner. In 1991 he received the Robert "Dutch" Huyser Award, the 21st Air Force Flight Engineer of the Year and the Military's Red-Carpet Award for Exceptional VIP Service.

He is a Co-author of the Chapter on International Protocol for the Convention Industry Council (CIC) International Manual, 1st Edition, 2005 (Co-contributors, Letitia Baldridge – White House, Dr. P.M. Forni – John Hopkins, and Alinda Lewris – Protocol and Etiquette Institute), and a Co-author, of the CIC Manual, 8th & 9th Edition, Chapter on "Etiquette, Ethics & Protocol" (with Colleen Rickenbacker – President Rickenbacker, Inc.).

He was selected as a consultant for the movie "Air Force

One," with Harrison Ford and has been ranked as one of the Top Five (5) Exhibit and Event Professionals worldwide by "Exhibitor Magazine." Mike received the Exhibit Marketer / Manager of the year by EXPO Group and E2MA, and Protocol Professional of the year by PDI-POA. He was recently selected by SPIN (Senior Professional Industry Network) as one of the top 40 over 40 event professionals worldwide.

Mike is sought after as a trainer, presenter and speaker at such Conferences as IAEE, EIC Conclaves, E2MA, TSTS, PDI-POA. He also mentor's individuals in Exhibitions, Events, Meetings and Protocol. He can be reached at: mdlspeaks@outlook.com